Haunted
FORT

The Spooky Side of Maine's Fort Knox

Liza Gardner Walsh

Down East
MAINE

Photographs © Jason P. Smith, except: East Coast Ghost Trackers, pgs 56, 61, 63, 65–68, 71;
State of Maine Department of Agriculture, Conservation, Forestry, Division of Parks and
Public Lands, pgs 20–26, 28, 31, 37, 41–47, 49–51; *Bangor Daily News*, pg 30; Matthew
Dolnack, pgs 60, 62: Bill Petrini pgs 38, 40; ©Oliver!|Dreamtime.com pg 6;
©Tashka|Dreamtime.com pg 12, ©Shutterstock pgs 2–3, 15, 17, 52, 55

Cover design by Rich Eastman
Book design by Lynda Chilton

ISBN: 978-1-60893-240-5

Printed in China

5   4   3   2   1

Down East
BOOKS·MAGAZINE·ONLINE
www.downeast.com

Distributed to the trade by National Book Network

Library of Congress Cataloging in Publication Data:

To Jeff,
my safety net

CONTENTS

Introduction ∞ 7

PART 1

Revolutionary Visions ∞ 13

The War of 1812 ∞ 15

The Site ∞ 16

The Silver Mine ∞ 19

Building the Fort ∞ 20

The Quarry ∞ 25

The Civil War ∞ 29

Luke Walker ∞ 31

Ordnance Sergeant Leopold Hegyi ∞ 34

The Spanish-American War ∞ 41

Fort Knox in the Twentieth Century ∞ 47

The Lost Fort ∞ 50

PART 2

Visitors' Stories ∞ 54

Today's Fort Keepers ∞ 63

The East Coast Ghost Trackers ∞ 65

Psychic Sisters ∞ 85

Fright at the Fort ∞ 91

Resources ∞ 96

About the Friends of Fort Knox ∞ 97

Acknowledgements ∞ 98

INTRODUCTION

Rising from the shore of the Penobscot River, Fort Knox is a sight to behold. The sheer size of the fort and the incredible workmanship it took to construct makes Fort Knox appear as the midcoast Maine version of the Great Pyramid. The fortified design is a taunt to enemies that never came — dare to enter, dare to fire, dare to take away America's freedom. The irony of Fort Knox is in what didn't occur — no enemy ever fired on it and no soldiers ever died in combat there. It is as if the splendor of Fort Knox itself is a ghost, a duplicitous sister fort, a possibility of what could have been. It is a representation of a bygone era in warfare — built a little too late, in a place a little too out of the way.

The history of the building of the fort and the climate of the country when it was commissioned is fascinating and will be briefly explored in this book. But it is the eeriness of Fort Knox that has emerged from its majestic beginnings that brings thousands of people to visit each year. Even the most skeptical among us have felt the heaviness of the air in Two-Step Alley and the sense that eyes follow as we walk through the officers' quarters. Even people who have never seen a ghost, or thought they ever would, have felt a cold pressure rubbing against their neck. And then there are those who come primarily to see the ghosts and to have a paranormal

experience led by professional ghost trackers committed to scientifically proving that the fort is indeed haunted.

But the question must be asked, What or who is haunting the fort? What makes the conditions so ripe for terror? According to Maine State Historian Tom Desjardin, there have been only three confirmed deaths at the fort. Two caretakers died on the premises and one German worker died of disease while stationed there. Are those three souls trapped inside? Is that what makes it one of the most haunted forts in America — haunted enough to be featured on a nationally syndicated television show? Or is it the confluence of swirling water, granite, and cold temperatures inside the fort that makes for perfect paranormal conditions? Who are these ghosts? Are they the spirits of the farmers who sold their land to the government so the fort could be built and who now search for their old homes? Is it one or both of the caretakers who strolled the grounds every day, morning and night, even in the dead of winter, even when there was no war in sight? Could they be spirits who traveled upriver from Castine, from the site of the most devastating naval disaster until Pearl Harbor — the Penobscot Expedition, where more than five hundred lives were lost? Could they be the ghosts of the young men who died at the Mount Waldo quarry preparing the stone to sheath the fort? Or the young man who died when the staging in the silver mine adjacent to the fort collapsed? Or the soldiers stationed there during the Civil War who deserted and were forced to come back? Who, who, who?

The first part will examine the theories behind the haunting of Fort Knox by looking at the history and the cast of characters involved in its more than two century existence. We will look at the changing roles of the fort and question whether the energy of these historical events has imprinted on the site, leaving haunted remnants. The second part will look at how all these elements and people coalesce to cast a spell on visitors. Stories from guests who never expected to see a ghost merge with those from psychics who specialize in spiritual contact. We will look at the detailed investigations of the East Coast Ghost Trackers, who have mapped out the key hot spots of paranormal activity within the fort, as well as the dominant

entities. Finally, we will see how this culture of haunting has fueled the renowned Fright at the Fort — the biggest fundraiser for the Friends of Fort Knox, the proceeds of which allow for the fort to be continually maintained.

As you read this, be forewarned that you may fall under the powerful and enchanting spell of Fort Knox. For anyone who has walked these ramparts cannot remain untouched by the grace of the fort. It is a tribute to skilled workmanship on a site that has witnessed more than two centuries of American stories. Whether you are a mystic, an aesthete, a historian, or a lover of the paranormal, Fort Knox offers itself to you.

PART 1

"During the American Revolution and again during the War of 1812, British Naval forces controlled the lower stretch of the Penobscot River. Fort Knox was built during the mid-nineteenth century to thwart a third British invasion that never came."

—FRIENDS OF FORT KNOX WEBSITE

VISIONS

During the American Revolution, in 1779, the British gained control of Castine, Maine, therefore controlling entry to the Penobscot River. The largest river in Maine, and second largest in New England, the Penobscot was the highway to and from Bangor, an important industrial and commercial area and the primary source for lumber and timber from Maine's northern forests. To control the mouth of this mighty river was to have a thumb on the valve of the economy. The Penobscot Expedition, which was the Americans' attempt to regain this strategic post, ended in a devastating loss. It was the largest military disaster until Pearl Harbor, with more than five hundred soldiers lost and forty-three ships sunk. According to historian John Cayford, "the Penobscot River became a Revolutionary War graveyard."

The site of Fort Knox was originally evaluated by General Peleg Wadsworth (grandfather of Henry Wadsworth Longfellow) and Colonel Paul Revere in 1779 for a defensive work if retreat was needed for the troops of the Penobscot Expedition. The remaining soldiers did indeed go into a retreat, but due to the Colonials' confusion after their loss, it was not at the future site of Fort Knox.

The question begs, did the spirits of these drowned soldiers travel? Did they watch in awe fifty years later as the magnificent fortification was built, wishing they could have hidden behind its sturdy walls during their trial at sea? Paranormal

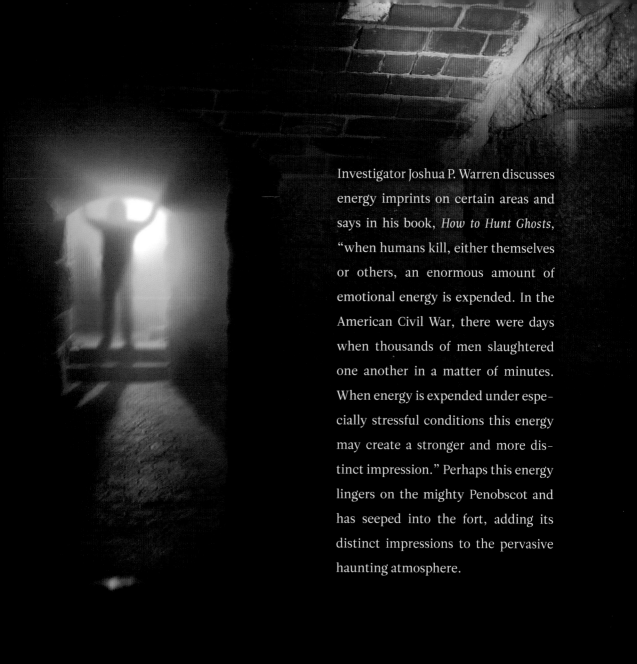

Investigator Joshua P. Warren discusses energy imprints on certain areas and says in his book, *How to Hunt Ghosts*, "when humans kill, either themselves or others, an enormous amount of emotional energy is expended. In the American Civil War, there were days when thousands of men slaughtered one another in a matter of minutes. When energy is expended under especially stressful conditions this energy may create a stronger and more distinct impression." Perhaps this energy lingers on the mighty Penobscot and has seeped into the fort, adding its distinct impressions to the pervasive haunting atmosphere.

THE WAR OF 1812

During the War of 1812, the British occupied and destroyed the countryside around the Penobscot River, proving again the vulnerability of this area to invasion and its importance in gaining access for trade. After America's defeat of Britain in 1812, the claims to the area did not hold and new borders were deter-

mined. The British claimed the entire upper valley of the St. John River and all of the land in Maine north of the forty-sixth parallel, which included about one-third of what is now the state of Maine. The Commonwealth of Massachusetts claimed land that ran well into New Brunswick and Quebec as far north as the St. Lawrence River. However, the borders remained in a state of fluctuation despite this designation, and the American government realized the need to protect this region from future attacks. In 1825, the United States' defense plans included a proposal for a fort at the current site of Fort Knox, but it took nearly twenty more years to get funding and to acquire the land.

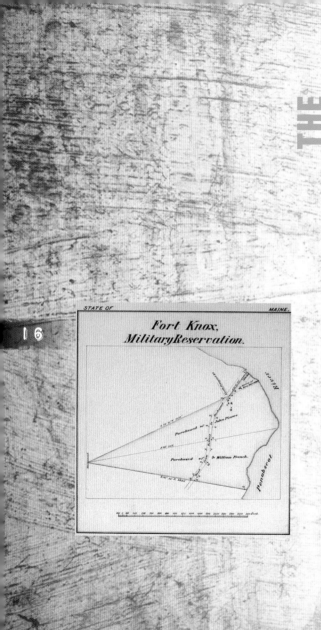

STATE OF   MAINE.

Fort Knox,
Military Reservation.

THE SITE

In 1840, the residents of Prospect, Maine, sent a resolution to Congress requesting protection. They were concerned about the proximity of Great Britain and the perpetually disputed border between Maine and British Canada — a border that was not completely solidified until 1842, when the Webster-Ashburton Treaty finally fixed the present boundary.

The request was received by the government, and on September 9, 1841, Congress appropriated twenty-five thousand dollars for a fortification to be built thirty miles north of Bangor, but a site was never selected. Two years later, after more citizen pressure, a congressional appropriation was passed on March 3, 1843, to relocate the fort to the Penobscot Narrows area and use the money previously appropriated for this project. At long last, the mighty Penobscot was to be protected and the residents collectively sighed with relief.

The United States Government obtained one hundred and twenty-five acres, ninety of which was woodlands, on the high ground on the west bank of the Penobscot River, opposite the town of Bucksport. The largest tracts were purchased from John Pierce and William French. John Pierce was a farmer and fisherman and his property was known as Pierce's Point. Smaller sites were purchased from Hannah

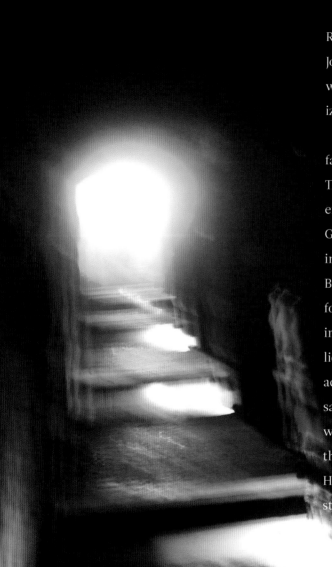

R. Harriman, Daniel H. Harriman, and John Lee. The total price of the purchase was $6,510 and the deeds were all finalized by March 23, 1844.

There is no record of what these farmers did after they sold their land. The Harrimans still owned property and operated the Prospect Ferry General Store. The Pierce family was involved in the masonry for the fort. But as we investigate the haunted fort, one wonders if this land is still impregnated with the love these families had for their farms. Despite their adherence to eminent domain for the safety of the country, did they just walk away, never looking back at those fields leading down to the river? Have their spirits returned, longing to stroll their property once again?

SILVER MINE

From 1838 to 1840, a silver mine was in operation on the shore of the Penobscot River, west of the designated site of Fort Knox. According to a special dispatch to the *Boston Globe*, "A young man named Samuel Batchelder, while in a shaft forty feet below the surface, was struck on the head by falling timbers. The accident will probably result fatally."

Silver mining at that time was dangerous and lacked basic safety regulations. Mining next to a river sometimes caused the mine shafts to flood. According to the Bureau of Geology, Natural Areas and Coastal Resources Website, "Due to mis-handling of explosives, potential cave-ins, poor air quality, and extreme weather conditions in the winter, digging these shafts was a dangerous business. They did it anyway in the hopes of future riches." But men like Samuel Batchelder would not see riches or even old age. Although his accident did not occur on the actual fort grounds, could his soul have become trapped in the mine? Or perhaps his restless spirit found the confines of the fort to be much like the underground place of his death and made itself at home.

BUILDING THE FORT

Finally, after years of government wrangling, construction began in May 1844 and Lieutenant Isaac Stevens, a young graduate of West Point and an engineer for the Corps of Engineers in the Coastal Survey Office, was put in command of the tremendous building project. He was responsible for surveying the land and laying out the design of the original fort. Taking the natural curve of the land into consideration, Stevens designed a mostly underground fort in the shape of a pentagon with front walls facing the river. The high ground in the rear of the fort served as an observation post and allowed for increased protection.

Many engineers and designers played roles in the evolution of one of the finest fortifications in the nation, but Lieutenant Stevens must be given the initial praise. His vision set the stage for this magnificent feat of engineering. He led the project

for the first three years of construction, then returned in 1850 after being promoted to captain and continued on the project for another three years. He proposed a very detailed schedule to complete the fort by 1856, with five annual appropriations of $75,000 and

Mt. Waldo Quarry

one for $65,000. Yet when construction stopped in 1869, not only was the fort still not completely finished, it had cost considerably more than Stevens's estimate of $475,000 — it eventually cost well over a million dollars.

In 1859, a reporter from the *Bangor Daily Times* wrote a story on the development of the fort, stating, "The works have been in progress for many years, and until within a year or two had made but little apparent outside show, besides the green embankments and the high, oblique iron-colored stone sustaining the shore wall. The massive works of the superior batteries are now partially completed, and the granite masonry

already bristles with grim port-holes." The reporter continues, describing the "green slopes which strike the eye externally with their smoothness and regularity, are the breastworks, over which, in case of need, black thunderers will point their saucy nozzles."

Stevens died in 1862, while fighting in the Civil War. He had been involved in many battles, engineering projects, and served as governor of Washington State, where he ruthlessly seized land from the Indians. Perhaps his spirit is still restless from so much military action and returns to the fort to continually check on its progress.

THE QUARRY

Cresting over one thousand feet tall, Mount Waldo, in the town of Frankfort, stands sentinel over Fort Knox like a proud mother, clothing the fort with her distinctive granite. Mount Waldo granite has a coarse-grained texture that gives it a patchy,

mottled look and was used in such famous landmarks as the Washington Monument, the Philadelphia Mint, the United Nations Building, and even the Empire State Building.

Excavation of the Fort Knox site began in July 1844. In 1848 more than

15,000 yards of stone was excavated, plus 10,000 yards of earth from the actual site. By 1851, seven years later, granite from Mount Waldo began to arrive on freshly laid rails. Flat cars on an endless chain ran on these rails and guided the blocks down the mountain, then as many as sixteen teams of oxen transported the slabs to the site.

The work was hard, dangerous, and required masonry training, but few stonecutters and quarry men worked in Maine at the time, so Governor John Hubbard went overseas to England and Ireland and recruited men to work the Fort Knox site. Many of the families of these men stayed after the project, making the Bucksport area their home. One of the expert stonecutters was a man named Captain Jefferson Watts, who was said to be able to fashion anything out of granite. Men who worked at the quarry were most likely paid about $1.05 a day for their back-breaking work. It is believed that several men died quarrying the stone for the fort. Official letters from Thomas Lincoln Casey, captain of the Corps of Engineers, discuss payments to the heirs of William W. Osgood and Charles H. Silsby of sums owed to them at the time of their deaths. Could these two skilled stoneworkers, who died while creating "Maine's Castle," have chosen Fort Knox as a final spiritual resting place?

THE CIVIL WAR

When the Civil War began, Fort Knox was still under construction, but it was needed for use as a training ground for the Union army. The number of soldiers during this time varied but was never large. The troops lived in temporary wooden buildings behind the massive unfinished fort. The first troops arrived in July 1863 from the 1st Maine Heavy Artillery Regiment, the 1st Maine Infantry Volunteers, and the 7th Maine Infantry Volunteers, comprising twenty-five men under the command of Lieutenant Thomas H. Palmer. Reinforcements arrived in September, bringing the number of men to fifty-three soldiers and one officer. Desertion crept in and three men fled the ranks in October, one in December, and two more in February. Imagine how cold it was living in those temporary barracks in the middle of a Maine winter, stuck training for months while many other soldiers were fighting and dying on the battlefield. What about the families left behind on farms with no man to help tend the fields or the animals? Desertion must have crossed the minds of many of these men and perhaps their spirits were forced back to the fort to suffer after death.

In 1865, 116 men were listed as on duty at the fort. That year a German soldier died of disease and was buried in an unmarked grave on the fort's property. He is one of the three confirmed deaths at the fort and perhaps is one of the soldiers

whose spirit still marches the parade grounds. By November 1865, the fort had only five men listed on active duty, and finally only the members of the Army Corps of Engineers stayed on to complete the fort.

LUKE WALKER

Little is known about Luke Walker, a caretaker of the fort commissioned a few years after the end of the Civil War. He served as caretaker for nine years, from 1871 until his death in 1880, and is one of the two caretakers who died there, thus he is a prime candidate for a ghost.

Walker was born in 1821 in Tarrytown, New York, and married an Irish woman named Catherine in 1845. He is described as having gray eyes, dark hair, and a dark complexion. He served in the military for forty-two years and upon his discharge in Fort Preble, Maine, was then commissioned to be the commander — and sole occupant — of Fort Knox, a position he held for the remainder of his life. During the nine years he and Catherine lived in the caretaker's cottage, their granddaughter lived with them. Her name was Ruth Eva O'Dea and she was one of nine siblings. Her grandparents took a shine to her and asked if she could live with them at the fort. Imagine living at the fort as a young child in the late nineteenth century and having the fort as your playground. Perhaps making rounds with your grandfather in the morning, then boarding the Totten Ferry with him to gather the news from Bucksport.

Luke Walker's cause of death was reported as an ulcerated liver, implying a lifetime of heavy alcohol consumption. Perhaps the fort drove him to drink, with the tedium and quiet of his post. Yet it seems as if his tenure was benign. The country was in stasis after a war that had forever changed the face of combat and made the fort itself outdated. His patrols were most likely uneventful as the fort slipped out of the government's interests. He had family nearby for companionship and perhaps young Ruth Eva joining him on the occasional rounds. He probably had a few drinks to help him wind down after lowering the flag. Perhaps the last years of his life were pleasant, maybe so much so that he still walks the fort. Maybe even holding young Ruth Eva's hand.

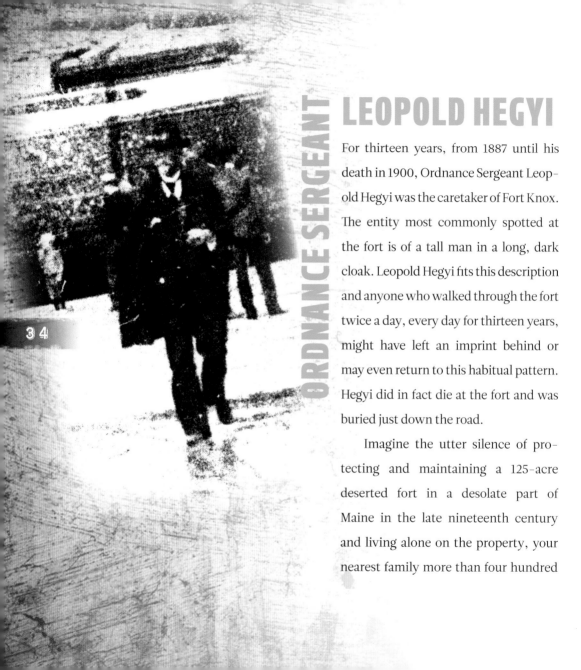

LEOPOLD HEGYI

For thirteen years, from 1887 until his death in 1900, Ordnance Sergeant Leopold Hegyi was the caretaker of Fort Knox. The entity most commonly spotted at the fort is of a tall man in a long, dark cloak. Leopold Hegyi fits this description and anyone who walked through the fort twice a day, every day for thirteen years, might have left an imprint behind or may even return to this habitual pattern. Hegyi did in fact die at the fort and was buried just down the road.

Imagine the utter silence of protecting and maintaining a 125-acre deserted fort in a desolate part of Maine in the late nineteenth century and living alone on the property, your nearest family more than four hundred miles away. Imagine the kind of man who could find solace in this solitary life and you have Ordnance Sergeant Leopold Hegyi. Historian John Cayford describes the pattern and loneliness of this post in the following passage:

> You woke at daybreak, washed, dressed, cooked breakfast, walked down to the fort and raised the flag, started a new daily report, then made a tour of inspection. There was not a single human voice to greet you while making your daily rounds. A few birds took flight from their nests when they heard your footsteps echo loudly on the granite floor. Small animals and rodents scurried at your approach. Your lantern cast weird shadows on the walls.

Every day, Sergeant Hegyi followed the same morning routine, then boarded a ferry — when the river was not frozen — and crossed into Bucksport to the post office to gather any military dispatches or letters from his wife, Louise, who lived in Brooklyn and visited twice a year with her two dogs. Hegyi then conducted an evening round, retracing his route through the fort, then lowering and folding the flag. When his work was completed, he walked down to the Prospect Ferry store for one daily beer and a glimpse of society. People admired this man and everyone was his friend. According to Cayford, "His bluish-gray eyes were always alert and sparkling: his iron-gray hair and white beard were always well trimmed; his uniform was clean

and impeccable, and those tall, black cavalry boots glistened as they were polished nightly. His conversation was light, but interesting, as Leopold was a well-read man." After his one beer, he would say to his companions, "Now I've got to go the hill up."

Leopold Hegyi was born on February 29, 1832, in Pest, Hungary, now Budapest. His education was considered decent and he was most likely involved in some form of animal husbandry. He fled Hungary after the Hungarian Revolution, which occurred during 1848 and 1849, when he was between eighteen and twenty years old. Within five years of joining the American army, he was promoted to sergeant. His rapid rise in the ranks, despite having to learn a new language and culture, shows that he was

extremely well-suited to the life of a military man. He was a decorated cavalry officer who trained horses for Custer's army in St. Louis, the gateway to the Wild West. He carried his love of horses with him while he was stationed at the fort and kept one in a stable across the river in Bucksport. During the winter, he attached skis to an old sawhorse and let the horse pull him around on the ice.

After ten years, when Hegyi was sixty-eight years old, a fort inspector was inspired to write a letter to head-quarters requesting that this "old sol-dier lay down his responsibilities by being transferred to the retired list." Headquarters denied the request and Hegyi was reenlisted for another three years, which he was unable to com-plete. A year after his reenlistment, in

1898, America found itself at war with Spain and the fort was occupied by 575 men from the First Regiment Connecticut Volunteer Infantry as well as U.S. Naval forces. With the occupation, the fort must have seemed like a foreign land to Hegyi, but given his friendly disposition, perhaps it was a welcome change. According to an exhibition panel in the Fort Knox Visitor Center, Hegyi was considered "an oracle to the men." But by the end of the summer, the troops were gone. The mines the navy planted were removed from the Penobscot River, deactivated, and stored at the fort, and the navy sailed away. Again, the only person left was Leopold Hegyi.

On July 16, 1900, a local fisherman noticed that the flag was not flying over the fort. He investigated and found Sergeant Hegyi gravely ill. When the doctor arrived, Hegyi was unconscious. His wife was notified and immediately left New York, but by the next day, Ordnance Sergeant Leopold Hegyi was dead. He was buried just down the road in Sandy Point, Maine, in the Narrows Cemetery, in a plot at the very back of the graveyard, close enough to the fort so he can continue to keep watch.

Perhaps the routine and the ability to read and contemplate was an ideal life for this man. Perhaps the granite walls of the fort heard him tell stories of his cavalry days and his childhood in Hungary. He was a strong admirer of the amazing workmanship of the fort, which reminded him of the quality stonework seen in his home country. The fort became a place of comfort, a substitute for family. Perhaps this kind, intelligent man didn't want to leave, even after death, and

today still makes sure that people take care of this invaluable edifice. Hegyi clearly loved the fort and the position gave him purpose. Entities are often those spirits who had a strong connection to a place and choose to stick around in that location. According to a renowned psychic, Leopold Hegyi does indeed still patrol the fort, with his stern but kind spirit serving as a father figure for the spirits of ghost soldiers trapped there. They are like sons to him, and he guides them, helping them cross over. Some of these men are not doing well, sudden deaths make them confused, and Leopold Hegyi, according to this psychic, helps them regain their memories and move on while he patiently walks his rounds, again and again.

THE SPANISH-AMERICAN WAR

During the Spanish-American War, residents up and down the East Coast reported visions of a Spanish ghost armada entering their harbors with guns blazing. These ghost vessels caused enough alarm that many forts were soon manned by volunteer troops. The citizens of Bangor petitioned Congress for protection and on June 10, 1898, the First Regiment Connecticut Volunteer Infantry was dispatched to Fort Knox, the guardian of the Penobscot Valley.

The towns of Bucksport and Prospect greeted the troops with fervor and a frenzied excitement overtook the communities. The regiment's band played, flags

flew, and Uncle Sam's soldiers crossed the river to their new home on the hilltop. Colonel Charles C. Burdette (inset p. 44) led the troops and was said to be one of the strictest disciplinarians in the volunteer army. His commands were obeyed to the letter. According to the local paper, the *Bucksport Commercial*, "The colonel is no trifler. He is hard on offenders and the rules here are like iron." But the troops believed Burdette looked out for their best

interests and that he took care of them well. Soon the fort became known as Camp Burdette. Hundreds of men slept in tents strewn along the green hillsides to prepare them for tent life if they were to head to Cuba to fight in the war.

The First Regiment Connecticut Volunteer Infantry arrived to a fort that by 1898 was deemed out of date due to the invention of long-range cannons. Again, the *Bucksport Commercial* declared, "While at the time of its construction the fortification was a powerful one, today it would probably make but little resistance to the modern guns, which could quickly blow it to pieces from a position several miles down the bay."

The fort was closed to all citizens during this occupation and guarded at all times "by a stalwart giant in blue standing there under a tersely worded signboard, rifle always ready to bar your progress." To people who previously enjoyed strolling the fort grounds, this was a downside of the occupation. But the influx of business and prosperity to the community was worth the trade-off. The local stores and

No PERSONS ALLOWED ACCESS TO THIS FORT EXCEPT PERMISSION OF THE ENGINEER OFFICER IN CHARGE.

several farms on the hill provided eggs, milk, and butter to the camp mess. Yet despite the increasing revenues, the same reporter from the *Bucksport Commercial* presents a wistful side to the inundation of troops in the following passage:

> "Prospect Ferry is not what it used to be. Still the sunshine bakes down on its slippery hill slope, still the Penobscot breezes sweep it clean and the northern sun shines brilliantly upon it. Still the old ferry steamer puffs back and forth, and patrons continue daily to clang the old bell in its antiquated frame to call her over from the Bucksport shore. Yet there is a new element there. The grass is trodden down under hundreds of feet. Hoarse voices and the clang of infantry echo through the groves that line the hills. The doors of the fort are thrown open. Rifles flash on the parapets and men shout in the batteries. Prospect, you see, is getting her share of the war. In truth, it must be said her people are profiting by it."

The profits, the bustle, and even the entrenched footprints trudging all over the property lasted less than two months. The well-ordered tent city was deconstructed as rapidly as it was built, and the soldiers again boarded trains south. Leaving behind only memories of a fort enshrouded by tents, troops, and the firm command of Colonel Charles Burdette, his orders echoing off the stone walls. Perhaps in death he still parades his troops through the fort, running the spirits with his iron fist raised up high.

46

THE TWENTIETH CENTURY

The State of Maine purchased Fort Knox from the United States Government in 1923 for $2,100. It was assigned to the State Park Commission in 1943. Athough there were several civilian caretakers, no one looked after it with the devotion of Leopold Hegyi. According to executive director of the Friends of Fort Knox, Leon Seymour, the fort was open with minimal supervision from the 1920s until the late sixties. People came to the fort for picnics, family reunions, and parties to revel on the riverside. Teenagers came for late-night drinking. Couples came to escape the eyes of their parents.

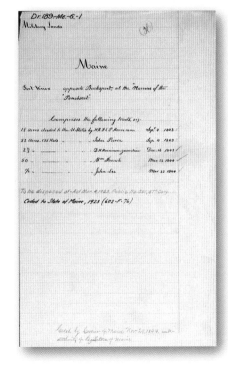

Did any of the activities at the fort during these years leave a ghostly imprint? According to Joshua Warren, an imprint is an "event that is recorded in the environment." He continues, "With an imprint, the location's history may play a more important role as well. An entity can move

about, but an imprint stays at the place it was made." Rumors abound of dark happenings at the fort during these years—rapes, fist fights, even the possibility of a murder. Although this is all unsubstantiated, the psychics and ghost hunters who regularly visit the fort confirm these speculations by picking up illicit and disturbed energy from these events.

The current visitor's center continually reinvented itself throughout the twentieth century. It served as a local diner with a small rooming house above in the 1930s. In the forties, the building was used as a one-room schoolhouse for the children of Prospect. When it was no longer needed for education, it became a maintenance facility for the state. In the fifties, the fort was used as a bomb shelter. Some say this building is also haunted, that its many shifting roles make it a strong candidate. Fort employee Amanda McDonald reports hearing the director's chair rocking, but when she called out she realized she was the only one in the building. Perhaps the ghost hunters will investigate this building, one of the remaining structures in a network of buildings that no longer exist.

THE LOST FORT

Underneath the layers of earth below the vast expanse of Fort Knox lies what Leon Seymour refers to as the "undiscovered Fort Knox." In 2009, archaeologist Peter Morrison began excavating and conducting two-week-long archaeological field schools. During these sessions, Morrison worked to unearth this "lost fort."

During the first field school, Morrison uncovered "two sets of artifacts that tell two different stories." The archaeologists uncovered pieces of window glass called "crown glass," which was a method of making glass panes common in the 1700s. These glass remnants were most likely from one of three residences that sat on the

land purchased by the government. Farm buildings, implements, wells, and residences from the 1700s through the mid-1800s decorated this property prior to
the fort and many of the remnants wait to be discovered. The other artifacts are
from what Morrison presumes to be a blacksmith shop most likely active during
fort construction. During the twenty-five years it took to construct the fort, more
than twenty buildings were strewn throughout the 125-acre property. "There was
a thriving little community here," says Seymour, "but the records are not very
exact. Many of these buildings appear in pictures taken of the Bucksport Historical Society and of the Connecticut troops in front of barracks that have long since
disappeared."

As ghost hunters search for the various spirits haunting the fort, archaeologists seek to uncover the hidden history. Peter Morrison says about this quest, "We're dealing with a puzzle with thousands of pieces, we don't have just one piece that explains everything. And part of the problem is that a lot of the pieces are missing."

PART 2

*Fort Knox stands at the confluence of swirling waters,
vast stores of granite, and a generally cold climate, all
triggers for hauntings.*

VISITORS' STORIES

Entering Fort Knox through heavy iron gates under a massive stone pediment feels as if you are heading into a labyrinth. The stone is smothered with years of rust and dripping lime. Mold paints the monotonous gray in a greenish pallor. This high above the Penobscot River there is always a breeze, the wind reinforcing the mournful mood of the fort. Footsteps echo on the perfectly pointed red brick and immediately the temperature drops.

There are hot spots of paranormal energy in this cavernous building and you need only rely on the hair on the back of your neck to know where those places are: Two-Step Alley and long alley; the officers' quarters; the casemates, where cannons once stood; and various storage rooms. Hundreds of visitors have felt this energy and experienced strange things while walking through the fort.

What is it about the fort that makes it a veritable ghost chamber? As we know, only three confirmed deaths have been reported, but dying at a location is not prerequisite to haunting it. Many experts in the field of paranormal research assert that there are conditions that make some places better for haunting than others. Certain geomagnetic forces converge to make a place susceptible to spiritual activity. Fort Knox stands at the confluence of swirling waters, vast stores of granite, and a generally cold climate, all triggers for hauntings. Other spiritual practitioners, called geomancers, claim the earth has "ley lines" that carry energy in a grid formation. According to practitioner David Yarrow, ley lines are "long-wave, extremely low frequency beams of earth energy that connect regional points of power." Maine has a ley line running directly through the state and ending at the Canadian island of Campobello. All of these elements together could make the fort a "warp." Joshua Warren says that a warp is a sort of "paranormal catchall." Warps defy

THE GHOST FAMILY PHOTO

This amazing photograph was taken by East Coast Ghost Trackers paranormal investigator Hannah Baird. The photograph was snapped at around three in the morning just under the entryway to the fort. The photo shows a cluster of spirits, including a little girl in a bonnet and a young boy. To the left of this group of entities stands a solitary figure in a black hooded cloak.

space and time and may create "portals through which an entity might be able to materialize, or gain some kind of access more easily and with more strength due to the thinned veil."

Is the fort resting on some hidden psychic trigger that when pulled allows for spirits to pass through and walk its vast chambers? Are the ley lines pointing right at a portal opening to mass haunting? Many of the visitors, fort employees, area psychics, and paranormal investigators believe this is so and in the following pages they share their stories.

On August 14, 2011, a man who had never seen a ghost or ever imagined that he would, entered the fort and was forever changed by what he witnessed. What follows is an email sent by Keith Rayeski to the Friends of Fort Knox describing his experience:

First, please allow me to introduce myself. I am not what many, even myself, might shake your head at and call crazy. I am nearly fifty-two years old, a retired New Hampshire state trooper and father of three. My profession made me a "facts" kind of person. If I do not see things for myself or see conclusive and even scientific evidence, I am not easy to convince. If I had not experienced what I did today, and had heard this account from another, I would chuckle and say, okay, you saw a ghost and that's a neat thing, good for you. I would be convinced the recounting was from a whack job! But today, at the north end of the Two-Step Alley from about fifteen yards, I saw an apparition. I cannot tell you if it was male or female. It happened suddenly and lasted only a second. I observed this apparition to be a white object that if it had legs, would stand about 5'8". I did not see a head or arms or legs. At first I thought it may have been a woman in a white nightgown, however, as I discussed what I saw with my girlfriend, added to my consideration, that men of the Civil War-era often wore long white nightdresses. This "object" appeared suddenly in the arched doorway and moved from my right to my left and disappeared. I went to the end of the

alley to see if there was anyone, another visitor, moving down that hall-way, but, when I arrived at the end of the alley and looked left, it was a solid brick wall. There was no place a human could have gone.

Another guest to the fort in October 2012 had a similarly strange experience but was able to capture a picture to confirm his paranormal suspicion. What follows is his account:

My name is Matthew Dolnack and I visited the fort this past Tuesday, October 23. As I was walking the alleys surrounding the dry moat, I heard footsteps behind me as I walked. Thinking they were echoes, I stopped, only to hear the footsteps continue for a few more seconds. This happened three separate times in Long Alley. I am positive no one was behind or in front of me as there were only a few people visiting the fort at that time. I carried on walking, not hearing the footsteps again. I asked the woman working at the gift shop if it was a common occurrence and she said all sorts of things happen at the fort, explaining how ghost hunters had investigated and deemed the fort haunted. I have seen the episode and it was the main reason I wanted to visit the fort.

I took pictures of the fort during my visit and when I returned home to the Pittsburgh area, I downloaded the photos, looking for

anything paranormal. Well, I think I caught something in a photo. In the photo there is something in the upper right-hand corner, near where the vaulted ceiling meets the wall. It wasn't there when I took the photo, and looks like it is illuminated, blocking out the features of the masonry behind it. Hopefully I caught something for more evidence of the fort being haunted.

ORBS: Spherical balls of energy, not visible with the naked eye but captured in photographs. Dave Juliano of theshadowlands.net, and a ghost hunter, defines an orb as "the energy being transferred from a source (i.e., powerlines, heat energy, batteries, people, etc.) to the spirit so they can manifest." The spherical shape is the most energy-efficient shape for a spirit to assume.

MISTS: Vaporous and nebulous masses that appear in photographs and often resemble smoke. Mists sometimes form outlines of bodies or faces. Joshua Warren states that "mists may be phantoms in a state of transition from one form to another."

BODIED APPARITIONS: Photographs displaying a part or all of a defined ghost. These are very rare but are the most exciting finds for a paranormal investigator. The most famous of these images is the Brown Lady of Raynham Hall in Britain. The face of a Native American seen in the left side of this window is also a prime example.

FORT KEEPERS

The employees of Fort Knox follow the legacy of generations of caretakers before them. They walk through the fort morning and night, checking for any damage and leading visitors through dark passageways, sharing the fort's history. If anyone is primed for a paranormal experience, it is this crew. Teddy Cooke is one such worker who had a power-

ful encounter several years ago after Fright at the Fort. Cooke worked as a tower and gate attendant at the fort, but during Fright at the Fort he took on the role of tech crew, controlling the fog, lights, and creepy audio tracks for the event. On the night that changed Teddy's idea of reality, he was shutting down the electrical effects and locking up. About this night, he says, "I was going to the upper level of the officers' quarters when I saw it — it was the back of a leg moving at the end of the hall." Thinking it was someone left behind from Fright, Teddy called out to say the fort was closed but that he would escort them out. There was only silence. Cooke climbed the steps leading to Two-Step Alley and saw the dark outline of someone walking down the alley. He described the vision as a "solid shadow." He

says that "about halfway down, I could see the figure of a person. There was a red floodlight at the other end and it clearly blocked out the light. I looked down for just a second and when I looked up again, there was nothing there all the way to the end of the alley. At this point, I'm still thinking it's a person. There are pillars all the way down the alley, and I thought they may have ducked behind there. I thought maybe someone was going to jump out and scare me." Checking each pillar carefully all the way down, he began to realize no one was there. "There's no way anyone could have gotten down the alley in that time," he said. "Up until I got out I thought it was a person. I don't know what it was. I got out of the fort as quickly as I could."

GHOST TRACKERS

"If immortality be untrue, it matters little whether anything else be true or not."

— H.T. Buckle

For the past several years on blustery autumn nights, The East Coast Ghost Trackers (ECGT) gather in the Fort Knox Visitor Center. Clad in camouflage pants, black shirts, and tactical vests, they set up their command center for the throngs of people signed up to partake in their guided ghost hunts. Their vests are filled with valuable ghost hunting equipment—EMF meters, which detect electro-magnetic

fields, full-spectrum cameras, laser flashlights that set green webbed traps for ghosts to walk through, and various ghost boxes that ride the radio bands searching for the white noise that allow ghosts to communicate.

The excitement and eagerness is palpable as the group prepares for the evening's exploits. Early guests filter in, unsure of what to expect — some have seen ghosts before, some are looking for a ghost story to share at the bar later that evening, and some are desperate for a connection with a spirit to confirm their growing sense of extra-sensory-perception. It is this building energy that co-founder Jamie Dube relies on as he takes his place as leader of the hunt. According to Dube:

There is a lot that goes on when conducting a ghost tour. A lot of getting paranormal results/evidence is what I like to call "energy manipulation." We have done so many ghost tours that I know what types of energies/people the entities want to interact with. When I pass out equipment to certain people there are reasons. I'm somewhat of a conductor with the energy and entities. On a ghost tour I place people in certain spots. Even my spot is crucial. Spirits are attracted to certain energy vibrations and auras. I make it easier for them to want to cooperate. Concentration in the group is another huge factor. That's where I come in with energy manipulation. I get everyone focused and placed. I work

close with the energy that I know the entities are attracted to. Higher energy is easier to work with than lower energy. Also on tours, everyone that comes in has a different level of energy, and I have to get a balance so the entities can communicate. I also have to read people and try to get everyone to let go of any negatives or doubts before I start a tour. One downer in the group can ruin the whole tour. I'm strict on a ghost tour because of this, and very quick to keep the focus with all those people during a tour. The manipulation is the people's concentrated energy focus on the act at hand. Once I get all this leveled off, then it's all about trust and cooperation on the entity's part. Not all entities are nice, but the spirits at Fort Knox are content, it seems for now, and eager for the contact. It's definitely a lot deeper than most know.

This intensity of energy belies the need for patience in pursuing spirits. For not every ghost hunt turns up an abundance of paranormal activity. Still, the ghost hunters are fierce in their determination to document the layers of evidence they've accumulated over the years. Most of the significant material they have uncovered is a direct result of hundreds of hours of investigation, and with each tour more evidence stacks up to confirm the haunted nature of the fort. They know the ins and outs of the fort and the various "hot spots," moving directly to those areas without

wasting any time. Ken Ort and Jamie Dube are the founders of the East Coast Ghost Trackers, and while other paranormal groups are welcome at the fort, this group donates all of the proceeds from its ghost hunts to the preservation of Fort Knox. They have also established a rapport with several of the entities that call the fort home and in so doing have determined that it is an intelligent haunt, one with distinct reactions that change depending on the group or the mood of the spirit. The group members consider themselves scientists seeking to prove there is life after death, and the fort is their primary laboratory.

Once Jamie has determined who will wield the mighty K2 sensors and EMF meters, gone over the fort rules,

EQUIPMENT NEEDED FOR A GHOST HUNT:

Basics:

Flashlight and Head Lamp

Extra Batteries

Notebook and Pens

Watch

Food and Water

Cell Phone (turned off so as not to interrupt the EMF detectors)

Walkie-talkies (if you are with a group)

Ghost-hunting Devices:

Compass: This can determine if the electromagnetic field is off, because if the needle is not pointing due north, or if it spins, a powerful field is interrupting.

Thermometer: Detects cold spots where a ghost may be located.

Electronic Field Meter or K2 Sensor

Video Camera

Digital Camera: Remove infrared and ultraviolet settings to take a full spectrum of light.

Infrared Meter: To detect sources of heat.

Audio Enhancer: A device that enhances low sounds.

Night-vision Scope: Allows a ghost hunter to see in the dark without the disturbance of white light.

Spirit Box or Ghost Box: A tool that searches AM radio bands to find white noise for the ghost to speak through.

Ovilus PX: A dictionary box that allows the ghost to speak, searching through more than two thousand word choices.

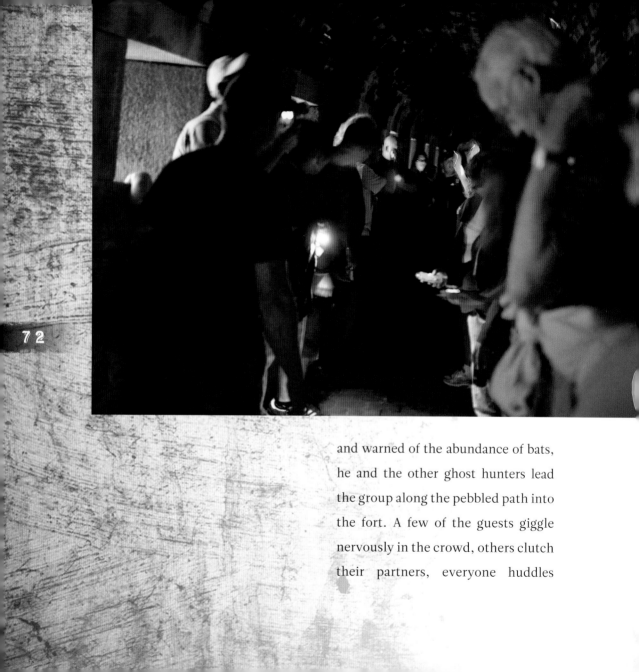

and warned of the abundance of bats,
he and the other ghost hunters lead
the group along the pebbled path into
the fort. A few of the guests giggle
nervously in the crowd, others clutch
their partners, everyone huddles

under warm layers of clothing, and no one knows what to expect. The fort is maze-like in the daytime, but at night all sense of borders is blurred and even if you are sure of where you entered, in no time you feel completely turned around.

The ECGT always start their tours in Long Alley, where a spirit known as "Mike" haunts. As we approach one of the wider casement areas, we are "placed" by Jamie, filling empty spaces and creating a web of bodies. Jamie pulls out his ghost box and asks Mike if he is here with us tonight. The static of the radio is jarring in this echo chamber and everyone cranes forward to listen as the radio attempts to detect a voice. "Mike, are you here with us? Finish my count, one, two..." and the waves of radio fluctuate until a clear word rings out, "apple." It seems Mike is a trickster and delights in provoking Jamie because as the interactions with Mike continue and Jamie asks, "What do you want us to do," a clear, albeit robotic voice emerges from the ghost box and says, "scram." Mike has clearly said people's names through the ghost box on other ghost hunts. Jamie reports that Mike prefers him to sit down, sometimes he obeys and sometimes he doesn't. But when he does sit, he can then usually get Mike to cooperate with him by manipulating the lights on the K2 meters, which is the next feat.

We follow Jamie back into the alleyway and line the sides. The brick is uneven in parts of this section and flashlights are needed, even as the apertures cut high in the granite walls let in tiny shimmers of moonlight. All of the people who have

74

received EMF and K2 meters are called to the top of the alley, where they hold their equipment up like magic wands. Some of the units are flashing green, but red means the electromagnetic field of a spirit is right there with us. The goal is for the benign green lights staring at us through the night like cat eyes to turn crimson. Jamie commands again, "Go to red, on the count of three." We wait, the suspense building as a cold breeze slides down the alley. One of the ghost hunters stationed next to me whispers that the breeze is a ghost. Ghost hunters refer to this as "an ionic breeze," when a ghost gathers particles to form a coldness that acts as wind. Just as Jamie says we are leaving since nothing is happening, all three lights immediately turn from

green to red. The crowd sighs collectively. Jamie says that tonight Mike is really playing with him, but somehow, it happened, the sensors were activated.

Jamie leads us up a set of stairs into a casemate area. The ECGT believe this area is home to an unintelligent haunt, a residual energy trapped in time. Last year they caught on infrared video a bar of light rising out of the floor and then moving from one wall to the other. The group theorizes that the imprinted energy is a remnant of something that happened in this area and is now trapped.

If there is time, the hunt will continue into the other paranormally charged alley — Two Step. Ken Ort and Jamie Dube believe an apparition that resembles

Hegyi often appears in this area. Jamie says that this figure is "strong as heck, powerful, and wants to be respected." It is this same entity that they saw standing on top of the fort looking down at them one night after a long ghost hunt. On other hunts, people have been "touched" in this area, hats knocked off, hair pulled, pant legs tugged, and cold air blown on the backs of their neck. On one tour, a woman standing in an archway screamed as she felt this touch. Interestingly, it is mostly women who are touched at the fort.

The premier stop on any ghost hunt is the area with the highest level of intelligent haunts — the officers' quarters. More paranormal experiences have occurred in this part of the

fort than anywhere else. Spirits seem to relish the wide-plank wooden floors and huge six-over-six lead glass windows. There is an exhibit in here that depicts what the room might have looked like when the First Connecticut Regiment was stationed at the fort in 1898. A cage surrounds the exhibit and a mannequin stares at you from its sedentary placement. The old pine-plank floor creaks, but that is not the only sound that is creepy, this area is where the ECGT have acquired most of their significant VPs — voice phenomena. Laughter, screams, and even what sounded like a cat shrieking have all been recorded in this area. Ghost tours have often been privy to the sound of footsteps in the upstairs quarters, and on a recent tour the footsteps sounded like they were walking among the group.

Poltergeist activity, which occurs when an entity moves an object, is common in this part of the fort. People have heard something that sounded like a rock being thrown above them, hitting the floor, and then rolling. Heavier things have thumped, like the sound of a trunk dropping. One time Jamie asked a spirit to move a wooden box in the exhibit and a half dozen people saw it shift a hair. The cage

containing the exhibit has rattled, as well as a plate inside the exhibit.

But people have also been touched in the officers' quarters. A teenager named Molly once felt something grab her elbow and pull her back into the room as she was trying to leave. She assumed it was her mother, but her mother wasn't near her. Amanda McDonald, a member of the East Coast Ghost Trackers and an employee at the fort, always gets a strong whiff of pipe tobacco when she enters this area. But perhaps the most profound contact the group has made with spirits was during the first ever Halloween night ghost investigation at the fort, when the veil between worlds is the thinnest. More than thirty people were witness to the night's powerful ghost activity. The following is the description from Jamie about what occurred that night in the officers' quarters.

At the same time Holly was with her group in the officers' quarters and having crazy contact, two women were physically touched and they had a medium/physic present in the group that Holly was working with. The medium told Holly and the group that there was a little girl there named Elizabeth. I did not find this out until last night about the little girl being picked up by the medium. This is where it gets crazy! I decided to combine both groups at the end for energy purposes and investigate in the officers'quarters one last time. It was just after midnight and the room was full. The K2 meters were dead, not doing a thing. I tried to bring out the cloaked man and was not having any luck. I then switched gears and decided to call on the children at the fort. The moment I started asking for the kids to come and play, the K2 meters started going crazy. I then asked the little girl entity that I felt there, if her name started with the letter B? The K2 started going crazy. I then asked her if her name started with the letter E? Again the K2 meter was going crazy. I then started calling her Elizabeth and started working with her name. I asked her if she was five years old to light the lights up five times in a row for me. She did, and more than once! I asked her if she had her mommy with

her? My dictionary device with over two thousand words programmed into it said "Mom."

I asked her if her mom would help her move something in the room for us. The device said "mommy." I asked Elizabeth if she would go over and give someone a hug. A woman from the group cried out in the pitch black, "Something is hugging me." Then another woman said, "Someone is holding my hand." I asked Elizabeth to make a noise so that we could hear her. We then could hear voices from upstairs. Also I found out last night that Holly's group heard the voices on the first investigation there earlier that night coming from upstairs. It was a very interesting night and amazing to have me and the medium hit on the name Elizabeth not knowing or speaking to each other. I think in time I will find out who these people are and maybe help them move on if they want.

As time goes on, the spirits in Fort Knox seem to be getting used to the idea of the ghost trackers, and with each investigation they reveal a little bit more of their mysteries. There is no doubt that this group has made contact with the entities that haunt the fort as they continue to scientifically attempt to prove that there is life after death.

AMANDA MCDONALD'S EXPERIENCES AS AN EMPLOYEE OF THE FORT AND AS A GHOST TRACKER

I started working at Fort Knox as a tour guide in 2011 and have enjoyed every moment of it. In my down time I wander the silent halls or gaze at the river from the roof. On my first day of work, I took some time to learn the elaborate maze. My first stop was Long Alley, dimly lit only by light coming in through the gun ports and separated from the main fort by a dry moat. Had there been a land invasion, the enemy's only access to the fort, other than through the main door, would have been to climb the steep hill leading right into the moat, where they would take fire from both sides. It was here that I had my first ghostly encounter. As I walked from the entrance to the alley and started up the hall, I got the feeling I wasn't alone — a feeling justified by what I thought were footsteps. As I began to turn around, I felt two taps on my shoulder. I continued turning, convinced I was about to see a person, but there was no one there and the alley was silent once more. The alley then leads into a series of small rooms called casemates, with arched ceilings and gun emplacements and dark dungeon-like rooms that were actually powder maga-zines. I later found out after a few hunts with the East Coast Ghost Trackers that these casemates are home to a man called Mike. He has a great record with us when it comes to intelligent spirits. He can send a fast cold breeze through the room on command, answer our counting questions, and produce large amounts of energy to light up all our EMF detectors.

I have found there to be activity regardless of the time of day. One of my tasks is to walk Two-Step Alley picking up trash before visitors arrive. Armed with not only a bucket and a trash grabber, I also bring my K2 meter. As soon as I turn it on and ask out loud, "Is there anyone who wants to help me clean this place up," the meter's lights start flashing all the way to the highest level. I make conversation and act casual and something keeps those lights lit up all the way through my rounds. I thought it might be a fluke at first, but I have noticed on the ghost tours that the meter doesn't go off in the same areas. I begin to wonder if a spirit is becoming too friendly with me and wants me all to himself. On recent ghost tours I have been the one to get responses over others in the group. Jamie, the leader of the ghost hunts, calls me the beacon, I think because I have an emotional connection to them now.

I have heard footsteps, running, and rocks being thrown and rolled. Once the steps were so hard on the floor above me that dirt from the ceiling of the officers' quarters fell on me. The same steps have followed me downstairs in the officers' quarters, even into a room full of people on a tour! In the morning in Two-Step, the footsteps can be heard echoing from Long Alley. I have also heard female and male screams, cat-like sounds, distant gunshots, and slamming doors. I will never figure out the slamming doors because the doors are all chained to the walls — and I have the key!

I have seen many shadows of humanlike figures dart from a dark room when I enter and I have seen them peering down curiously at us from the roof. My favorite thing to do is to go into the left side officers' quarters at night and stare at the tall slender windows. If you watch from the opposite end you will start to see them moving about. At first it seems your eyes are playing tricks on you because the moonlight from outside gets somewhat blocked out in the corners, but, then, if you're lucky, you'll see the entire window get blocked out, just for a second before they move again. It is one of the neatest things I have seen yet!

Even the visitor's center, although not as old or historically important as the main fort, has its own activity. After Leon has gone home and locked his office for the day, I sometimes hear his chair still squeaking, like someone is spinning it around. And a stuffed bear head wearing a Union cap hangs over the door to the gift shop. That hat sat on the bear's head from the day he went up, but one day, as a visitor was walking in, the cap fell right onto his head.

I have never been so intrigued and in love with a place. When I am there I am at peace. The walls and lands are full of spirits, a positive thing to be respected, not feared. Something about the fort has grabbed me, and it has a special place in my heart, as do the spirits within because they really are what makes the fort such a wonderful place.

PSYCHIC SISTERS

Sisters Sky Taylor and Amy Burgoyne are both gifted psychics with a strong connection to Fort Knox. They have had psychic encounters at the fort for more than ten years, never once visiting without something significant

occurring. Since their first visits as teenagers, they have always had the feeling that the place was spiritually active. They attest that the fort's energy is intense, almost like a vortex, and both have a wealth of stories about the various apparitions and spirits that fill the fort.

Over the past several years, Taylor and Burgoyne have participated in the fort's annual paranormal/psychic fair, where dozens of psychics and healers gather for the weekend. The duo also leads a new festival at the fort called the Healing Co-op Holistic and Wellness Fair. Sky hosted a radio show and did a live broadcast from the fort. During the broadcast she included the story from a former Fort Knox tour guide who reported that while giving a tour, a soldier showed up at the edge of the group. Civil War re-enactors often held encampments at the fort, so

the guide assumed this was the case. She discovered later that none of the re-enactors were at the fort that day. When she saw a photo of Sergeant Leopold Hegyi, she said the "ghost soldier" looked just like him.

On the night of the broadcast, while Sky and her husband were locked in the fort, any doubts that the fort was teeming with paranormal activity were forever squelched. While they were investigating the upstairs of the officers' quarters, they heard a loud boom, as if someone had stomped or slammed a door. Later, they heard one of the large wooden doors that shut off the alleys slam shut, but when they went to check, the door was chained open. Sky snapped several pictures that night, one of which showed a large black orb traveling down Long Alley and another showed a veil of mist, which if examined closely seems to take the form of a soldier.

I met Sky and Amy at the fort one day and they offered to lead me on a psychic tour. We began in the most active hot spot, the officers' quarters. We stood toward the back of the room, behind the exhibit, and immediately Sky began hearing whistling. She then hummed the tune that had come to her, "Did you ever see a dream walking, I did." The lyrics to this song from 1933 were very popular during that time period. As she sang, Amy said, "We have an audi-

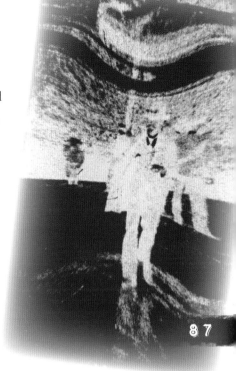

ence," and both women identified a group of people of all ages in 1930s-style clothing, similar to the photo captured by the East Coast Ghost Trackers of the ghost family. The man in the cloak from that photo was present, according to Sky. These spirits came often to picnic and enjoy the grounds and their experiences were imprinted, making them residual haunts. Sky even told us what they usually had for their picnics—mashed potatoes and chicken. The tall cloaked man had an air of considerable wealth and importance and both women felt he was involved in bootlegging, storing his wares in the fort. Now he is here to protect them in death.

Amy walked into the storeroom to the left of where we were standing, a dank, rough-hewn room with a dirt floor. She was immediately disturbed by the energy and declared that something really traumatic happened there — a woman was beaten and her spirit is trapped here. Amy was visibly shaken by this dark, sad energy and was reminded of how many of these events might have imprinted when the fort was wide open to the public.

We moved to the other side of the officers' quarters and sat on the long bench next to a fireplace, the only piece of furniture in this spartan room. Both women believe the spirit of Leopold Hegyi often resides here where military officers most likely conducted business. But as we sat, the spirits of several other officers seemed to join us and they both sensed one in particular that seemed quite ornery. Amy immediately heard him say, "bastard," over and over. Could this be the spirit of the serious and stern Colonel Charles Burdette from the First Connecticut Regiment, the iron-fisted leader?

In Two-Step Alley, Amy and Sky both reported tightness in their chests as the energy built. To Sky, the alley has a quality of an old filmstrip. As we descended the redundant two steps, Amy concurred, adding that it had a blurred quality. When we entered Long Alley, Sky heard a clear voice saying, "You better watch it. I can throw you right in here." The spirit is referring to one of the many small, windowless storage rooms set off the alley. Amy envisioned a man with hands on his hips, a disciplinarian, someone not scary, but firm. Sky reported that her leg felt "like a freezer," and both women again felt tension in their throats and ringing in their ears. Sky's head felt as if she were holding it with her hands on either side and shaking it, which Amy connected to an earlier vision she'd had of a head-injured spirit. The entire journey was like this, as the sisters wove their sensory perceptions seamlessly between each other, finishing the other's thoughts—sister energy compounding their psychic gifts. These women walk the thin line between our world and the world of spirits, and for them the place where the line is most permeable and close to the surface is at Fort Knox.

FRIGHT AT THE FORT

Every Halloween for more than thirteen years, the Friends of Fort Knox (FOFK) has created one of the most terrifying and well-designed haunted houses in New England, but be forewarned: Fright at the Fort is not for the faint of heart. The FOFK spend hundreds of hours setting up for this event and it is their biggest special event fundraiser of the year. The Fright attracts an average of eight thousand people and raises more than $50,000 for the fort to continue its preservation efforts.

On a surprisingly warm but wet October night we arrived at the fort shrouded in coastal fog. Lines of people fanned the circular driveway, where a "ghost buster" car was parked, complete with full ghost-busting regalia. High school students talked loudly with their friends, young couples cleaved to each other, and families attempted to entertain their older children—all waiting for the thrill of a good scare and a romp through a maze of zombies. Entering the visitor's center, we were met by the haunting sound of an organ, the organist decked out in a *Phantom of the Opera* mask and cape. Because we ordered express tickets, we were whisked to the front of the group, a vulnerable spot indeed. As we walked toward the fort dressed in its Halloween garb, our position was immediately challenged as three chainsaw-wielding zombies stormed us, raising their blades in our faces. No sooner did they back off than another mob of zombies met us at the heavy gates, warning us that this was our last chance to leave. Once inside, it would be too late.

But onward we plunged into the abyss, where a young woman hung, her hands suspended from the entrance, seemingly dead, but as we passed, she jerked alive and glared at us. From that moment on, zombie actors besieged us on our path—clown zombies, zombies in Hazmat suits, doll zombies. You can't help asking, where do these people come from? Who applies pounds of make-up to create a bludgeoned face or a hemor-rhaging chest wound pooling blood on a polka dot clown suit? It is these actors who truly make the Fright so successful. They hail from all over the midcoast area to become one of the "undead." Such as members of the

Searsport Drama Club, who have been volunteering since the very first Fright. The contrast between the wildly exuberant zombies who jump out at you from around hidden bends and the sullen catatonic corpses strewn in corners keeps you on your toes. You never know if a body in the corner is alive or if it is a mannequin, if that person huddled beneath a coffin will turn toward you at any moment and scream in your face.

Dripping wet stairwells lined with mud make walking treacherous and the maze-like alleys are further distorted by strobe lights, breaking up an already limited vision. Between watching your step on the uneven terrain and guarding against possible zombie incursions, your hackles are consistently raised through-out the journey. It is this sense of variation and confusion that makes the Fright so effective. At one point, the brick and granite tunnel transforms into a horse-shoe-shaped corn maze. The smell of rotting corn is stifling, but even worse is the surprising sight of a person's head leering at you through the stalks. Several other people are woven within the maze and their hands reach out as you wind your way, feeling as if trapped in the horror movie *Children of the Corn*.

In Long Alley, zombie baby dolls are set in the apertures while a steady stream of living zombies unsettle the group's order. There are areas in the Fright that defy normal expectations of a haunted house and are so laboriously crafted that you cannot help admiring the mad genius behind the installations. The pig butcher

shop is an example of an installation that gets better every year. For the 2012 event, a prop was procured from California and arrived on a flatbed truck, but if you hesitated to gape at this pig horror, a small plastic bloody pig might be thrown at you by one of the actors.

Everything moves fast at Fright and the ride is over before you know it. Suddenly you are vaulted out of the alley onto the terreplein, the fresh air and the night sky startling in their normalcy, the grass a stark contrast to the brick and stone. The sudden quiet more alarming than any zombie's scream.

Fright at the Fort is a production of the finest sort — a calibrated, multi-layered extravaganza leaving no terrifying stone unturned. Your heart will race, your step will fumble, you will

clutch someone's hand and cover your eyes. You may scream at times and laugh at others, but you will, no matter what, be deeply entertained. Yet, as spooky as the Fright is, it is the fort as stage that holds all the power. The truth is, that as dolled up as the fort gets for this event, it is far creepier in its bareness and silence. Once the zombies all pack up and go home and the props are put away for another cold winter, the fort quietly regains the spookiness that is the stuff of legend.

RESOURCES

East Coast Ghost Trackers

ghosttracking.com

The Healing Co-op — A holistic center
that offers reiki, intuitive guidance,
and massage. Amy Burgoyne (207-478-
8725) and Sky Taylor (207-659-2733),
thehealingco-op.com

How to Hunt Ghosts: A Practical Guide
by Joshua P. Warren

Fort Knox: Fortress in Maine
by John E. Cayford

ABOUT THE FRIENDS OF FORT KNOX:

The Friends of Fort Knox believe that by working in partnership with creative local organizations, the fort will become a historic resource and a venue for midcoast Maine talent. A summer-long series of historic reenactments, seminars, music, drama, local craft work, and art, makes the fort a must-see destination for local residents and tourists alike.

The Friends of Fort Knox have mobilized statewide support to save Maine's most popular state historic site using volunteer labor, in-kind donations, and grassroots fundraising.

The fort is in need of serious repair and upkeep in which state and local funds are not available for the extent of such work. Fort Knox belongs to all of us. We all need to preserve some of our few precious sites and heritage in which we experienced the joy and awe, so our children can do the same.

Please come visit Fort Knox, you won't forget the breathtaking experience and please support Friends of Fort Knox *(fortknox.maineguide.com/fofk.html)* so future generations will have a chance to visit the fort.

ACKNOWLEDGEMENTS

I have always loved history and ghost stories but might not have had the opportunity to combine the two if Michael Steere hadn't asked me to write this book. Thank you, Michael, for trusting me with this story and being patient as it unfolded. Thank you to everyone at DOWN EAST for all your hard work, especially Terry Bregy, Linda Callahan, Jan Dehn, Julie Boyer, Sue Smith, and Lynda Chilton, who truly brought the book to life.

So many people helped me with the research for this project. First, I couldn't have written anything without the kind, humorous, and wise advice from director Leon Seymour. Leon gave me tips to go on and laughs to help on the journey. I am grateful to John Cayford for his excellent book, *Fort Knox: Fortress in Maine*.

Maine State Historian Tom Desjardin, who doesn't even believe in ghosts, allowed me to ransack his files and take over his office for a day. The images he provided formed the backbone of the historical section of this book. Thank you to Jason Smith for your beautiful photos of the fort. Thank you also to Keith Rayeski, Matt Dolnack, and Teddy Cooke for allowing me to publish your stories.

My deepest thanks go to the East Coast Ghost Hunters, who allowed me to follow along on more ghost hunts than I can count and patiently answered my millions of questions. The entire group was so warm and fun that a ghost would be crazy not to show itself to them. Thank you especially to Ken Ort, Jamie Dube, and Amanda McDonald.

Heartfelt gratitude goes to Sky Taylor and Amy Burgoyne, who opened up their psychic door for me and shared such profound visions about the spirits at the fort. Thank you, Sky, for your words of wisdom during my final stretch of writing.

Thank you to the wise and kind Sandra Bart Heimann, who helped me to understand Sergeant Leopold Hegyi and appreciate him in a way I never could have without her insight. Her amazing retreat allowed the book to finally find its footing. Thank you also to the Meil family for sharing your Portland digs where the book truly came together.

My family was ever patient with me as I wrote, researched, and dragged them to the fort over and over. Thank you to Jeff, who embraced our ghost hunting "dates" and made them fun and memorable, and to Daphne and Phoebe, my great editors and ghost radar enthusiasts.

But the fort itself receives my largest praise. I feel lucky to have fallen under its spell.